Planning for Learning through
What are things made from?

by Rachel Sparks Linfield and Emiko Ray   Illustrated by Cathy Hughes

Contents

Published by Step Forward Publishing Limited
25 Cross Street, Leamington Spa CV32 4PX Tel: 01926 420046 www.practicalpreschool.com
© Step Forward Publishing Limited 2003

Planning for Learning through What are things made from? ISBN: 1 902438 96 5

Making plans

Why plan?

The purpose of planning is to make sure that all children enjoy a broad and balanced curriculum. All planning should be useful. Plans are working documents that you spend time preparing, but which should later repay your efforts. Try to be concise. This will help you in finding information quickly when you need it.

Long-term plans

Preparing a long-term plan, which maps out the curriculum during a year or even two, will help you to ensure that you are providing a variety of activities and are meeting the statutory requirements of the *Curriculum Guidance for the Foundation Stage* (QCA, 2000).

Your long-term plan need not be detailed. Divide the time period over which you are planning into fairly equal sections, such as half terms. Choose a topic for each section. Young children benefit from making links between the new ideas they encounter so as you select each topic, think about the time of year in which you plan to do it. A topic about minibeasts will not be very successful in November!

Although each topic will address all the learning areas, some could focus on a specific area. For example, a topic on 'What are things made from?' would lend itself well to activities relating to Creative Development and Knowledge and Understanding of the World. Another topic might particularly encourage the appreciation of stories. Try to make sure that you provide a variety of topics in your long-term plans.

Autumn 1	Nursery rhymes
Autumn 2	Autumn/Christmas
Spring 1	What are things made from?
Spring 2	Spring
Summer 1	Food
Summer 2	Minibeasts

Medium-term plans

Medium-term plans will outline the contents of a topic in a little more detail. One way to start this process is by brainstorming on a large piece of paper. Work with your team writing down all the activities you can think of which are relevant to the topic. As you do this it may become clear that some activities go well together. Think about dividing them into themes. The topic of 'What are things made from?', for example, has weekly themes such as 'Materials around us', 'Wood', 'Paper and card', 'Fabric and wool' and 'Shiny materials'. At this stage it is helpful to make a chart. Write the theme ideas down the side of the chart and put a different area of learning at the top of each column. Now you can insert your brainstormed ideas and will quickly see where there are gaps. As you complete the chart take account of children's earlier experiences and provide opportunities for them to progress.

Refer back to the *Curriculum Guidance for the Foundation Stage* and check that you have addressed as many different aspects of it as you can. Once all your medium-term plans are complete make sure that there are no neglected areas.

Day-to-day plans

The plans you make for each day will outline aspects such as:

- resources needed;
- the way in which you might introduce activities;
- the organisation of adult help;
- size of the group;
- timing;
- key vocabulary.

Planning for Learning through *What are things made from?*

Practical Pre-School

Making plans

Identify the learning that each activity is intended to promote. Make a note of any assessments or observations that you are likely to carry out. On your plans make notes of activities that were particularly successful, or any changes you would make another time.

A final note

Planning should be seen as flexible. Not all groups meet every day, and not all children attend every day. Any part of the plan can be used independently, stretched over a longer period or condensed to meet the needs of any group. You will almost certainly adapt the activities as children respond to them in different ways and bring their own ideas, interests and enthusiasms. The important thing is that the children are provided with a varied and enjoyable curriculum that meets their individual developing needs.

Using the book

● Collect or prepare suggested resources as listed on page 21.

● Read the section which outlines links to the Early Learning Goals (pages 4-7) and explains the rationale for the topic of 'What are things made from?'.

● For each weekly theme two activities are described in detail as an example to help you in your planning and preparation. Key vocabulary, questions and learning opportunities are identified.

● The skills chart on page 23 will help you to see at a glance which aspects of children's development are being addressed as a focus each week.

● As children take part in the 'What are things made from?' topic activities, their learning will progress. 'Collecting evidence' on page 22 explains how you might monitor children's achievements.

● Find out on page 20 how the topic can be brought together in a grand finale involving parents, children and friends.

● There is additional material to support the working partnership of families and children in the form of a 'Home links' page, and a photocopiable parent's page at the back of the book.

It is important to appreciate that the ideas presented in this book will only be a part of your planning. Many activities that will be taking place as routine in your group may not be mentioned. For example, it is assumed that sand, dough, water, puzzles, floor toys and large scale apparatus are part of the ongoing pre-school experience, as are the opportunities which increasing numbers of groups are able to offer for children to develop ICT skills. Role-play areas, stories, rhymes and singing, and group discussion times are similarly assumed to be happening each week although they may not be a focus for described activities.

Using the Early Learning Goals

Having chosen your topic and made your medium-term plans you can use the *Curriculum Guidance for the Foundation Stage* (QCA, 2000) to highlight the key learning opportunities your activities will address. The Early Learning Goals are split into six areas: Personal, Social and Emotional Development; Communication, Language and Literacy; Mathematical Development; Knowledge and Understanding of the World; Physical Development and Creative Development. Do not expect each of your topics to cover every goal but your long-term plans should allow for all of them to be addressed by the time a child enters Year 1.

The following section highlights parts of the *Curriculum Guidance for the Foundation Stage* in point form to show what children are expected to be able to do in each area of learning by the time they enter Year 1. These points will be used throughout this book to show how activities for a topic on 'What are things made from?' link to these expectations. For example, Personal, Social and Emotional Development point 7 is 'form good relationships with adults and peers'. Activities suggested which provide the opportunity for children to do this will have the reference PS7. This will enable you to see which parts of the Early Learning Goals are covered in a given week and plan for areas to be revisited and developed.

In addition, you can make sure that activities offer variety in the goals to be encountered. Often a similar activity may be carried out to achieve different learning objectives. For example, during this topic the children will use paper and card shapes to make pictures and patterns. The children will be developing mathematical language, using words such as 'circle' or 'bigger' but they will also be exploring colour, texture, shape, form and space (Creative Development) and looking closely at similarities and differences (Knowledge and Understanding of the World). It is important, therefore, that activities have clearly defined goals so that these may be emphasised during the activity and for recording purposes.

Personal, Social and Emotional Development (PS)

This area of learning covers important aspects of development that affect the way children learn, behave and relate to others.

By the end of the Foundation Stage, most children will:

PS1   continue to be interested, excited and motivated to learn

PS2   be confident to try activities, initiate ideas and speak in a familiar group

PS3   maintain attention, concentrate and sit quietly when appropriate

PS4   have a developing awareness of their own needs, views and feelings and be sensitive to the needs, views and feelings of others

PS5   have a developing respect for their own cultures and beliefs and those of other people

PS6   respond to significant experiences, showing a range of feelings when appropriate

PS7   form good relationships with adults and peers

PS8   work as part of a group or class, taking turns and sharing fairly, understanding that there needs to be agreed values and codes of behaviour for groups of people, including adults and children, to work together harmoniously

PS9   understand what is right, what is wrong, and why

PS10   dress and undress independently and mange their own personal hygiene

PS11   select and use activities and resources independently

PS12   consider the consequences of their words and actions for themselves and others

PS13   understand that people have different needs, views, cultures and beliefs, that need to be treated with respect

PS14   understand that they can expect others to treat their needs, views, cultures and beliefs with respect

Practical Pre-School

The topic of 'What are things made from?' offers many opportunities to contribute to children's personal, social and emotional development. Time spent discussing what materials feel like, their appearance and how they are used will encourage children to speak in a group, to be interested and to consider consequences. By joining in circle times children will learn to take turns and understand the need for agreed codes of behaviour. Many of the areas outlined above though, will also be covered as children carry out activities designed to support other areas of learning. During undirected free choice times they will be developing PS11 whilst any small group activity that involves working with an adult will help children to work towards PS7.

Communication, Language and Literacy (L)

The objectives set out in the *National Literacy Strategy: Framework for Teaching* for the Reception year are in line with these goals. By the end of the Foundation Stage, most children will be able to:

L1   enjoy listening to and using spoken and written language, and readily turn to it in their play and learning

L2   explore and experiment with sounds, words and texts

L3   listen with enjoyment and respond to stories, songs and other music, rhymes and poems and make up their own stories, songs, rhymes and poems

L4   use language to imagine and recreate roles and experiences

L5   use talk to organise, sequence and clarify thinking, ideas, feelings and events

L6   sustain attentive listening, responding to what they have heard by relevant comments, questions or actions

L7   interact with others, negotiating plans and activities and taking turns in conversation

L8   extend their vocabulary, exploring the meaning and sounds of new words

L9   retell narratives in the correct sequence, drawing on language patterns of stories

L10   speak clearly and audibly with confidence and control and show awareness of the listener, for example by their use of conventions such as greetings, 'please' and 'thank-you'

L11   hear and say initial and final sounds in words and short vowel sounds within words

L12   link sounds to letters, naming and sounding letters of the alphabet

L13   read a range of familiar and common words and simple sentences independently

L14   show an understanding of the elements of stories such as main character, sequence of events, and openings, and how information can be found in non-fiction texts to answer questions about where, who, why and how

L15   know that print carries meaning, and in English, is read from left to right and top to bottom

L16   attempt writing for different purposes, using features of different forms such as lists, stories and instructions

L17   write their own names and other things such as labels and captions and begin to form sentences, sometimes using punctuation

L18   use their phonic knowledge to write simple regular words and make phonetically plausible attempts at more complex words

L19   use a pencil and hold it effectively to form recognisable letters, most of which are correctly formed

A number of the activities suggested for the theme of 'What are things made from?' are based on well-known picture books and stories. They allow children to enjoy sharing the books and to respond in a variety of ways to what they hear, reinforcing and extending their vocabularies. Throughout the topic, opportunities are described in which children are encouraged to use descriptive vocabulary and to see some of their ideas recorded in both pictures and words as they collaborate to write a poem about playdough and make big books and posters.

Mathematical Development (M)

The key objectives in the *National Numeracy Strategy: Framework for Teaching* for the Reception year are in line with these goals. By the end of the Foundation Stage, most children should be able to:

M1   say and use number names in order in familiar contexts

M2   count reliably up to ten everyday objects

M3   recognise numerals one to nine

M4   use language such as 'more' or 'less' to compare two numbers

M5   in practical activities and discussion begin to use the vocabulary involved in adding and subtracting

M6   find one more or one less than a number from one to ten

M7   begin to relate addition to combining two groups of objects and subtraction to 'taking away'

M8   talk about, recognise and recreate simple patterns

M9   use language such as 'circle' or 'bigger' to describe the shape and size of solids and flat shapes

M10   use everyday words to describe position

M11   use developing mathematical ideas and methods to solve practical problems

M12   use language such as 'greater', 'smaller', 'heavier' or 'lighter' to compare quantities

The theme of 'What are things made from?' provides a meaningful context for mathematical activities. Children are given opportunities to explore shapes and size as they collaborate to cut fruits for a rice salad, make tartans and use shapes for collages. Children can count as they stick shiny things on to numbers and count the rainbow fish's shiny scales. Children use wooden objects to measure lengths. The jumble sale is a wonderful opportunity for children to gain awareness of coins, to buy, sell, sort and count.

Knowledge and Understanding of the World (K)

By the end of the Foundation Stage, most children will be able to:

K1   investigate objects and materials by using all of their senses as appropriate

K2   find out about, and identify, some features of living things, objects and events they observe

K3   look closely at similarities, differences, patterns and change

K4   ask questions about why things happen and how things work

K5   build and construct with a wide range of objects, selecting appropriate resources and adapting their work where necessary

K6   select the tools and techniques they need to shape, assemble and join materials they are using

K7   find out about and identify the uses of everyday technology and use information and communication technology and programmable toys to support their learning

K8   find out about past and present events in their own lives, and those of their families and other people they know

K9   observe, find out about and identify features in the place they live and the natural world

K10   begin to know about their own cultures and beliefs and those of other people

K11   find out about their environment, and talk about those features they like and dislike

The topic of 'What are things made from?' offers many opportunities for children to make observations, to ask questions and to compare. As they explore the texture of materials they are encouraged to notice details. Activities such as investigating mirrors and tapping pieces of wood will encourage children to use their senses. Through all the activities children are encouraged to talk and to give reasons for choices and observations.

Physical Development (PD)

By the end of the Foundation Stage, most children will be able to:

PD1   move with confidence, imagination and in safety

PD2   move with control and coordination

PD3   show awareness of space, of themselves and of others

PD4   recognise the importance of keeping healthy and those things which contribute to this

PD5   recognise the changes that happen to their bodies when they are active

PD6   use a range of small and large equipment

PD7   travel around, under, over and through balancing and climbing equipment

PD8   handle tools, objects, construction and malleable materials safely and with increasing control

Activities such as using clay, dough and construction toys will offer experiences of PD8. Through pretending to travel and go to a jumble sale children will have the opportunity to move with control and imagination. Through using a range of small equipment such as bean bags and travelling between paper flags, children will be encouraged to develop their coordination and control.

Creative Development (C)

By the end of the Foundation Stage, most children will be able to:

C1   explore colour, texture, shape, form and space in two or three dimensions

C2   recognise and explore how sounds can be changed, sing simple songs from memory, recognise repeated sounds and sound patterns and match movements to music

C3   respond in a variety of ways to what they see, hear, smell, touch and feel

C4   use their imagination in art and design, music, dance, imaginative and role play and stories

C5   express and communicate their ideas, thoughts and feelings by using a widening range of materials, suitable tools, imaginative and role play, movement, designing and making, and a variety of songs and musical instruments

During this topic, children will experience working with a variety of materials as they make collages of scenes and the queen's knickers. They will be able to develop their imaginations and skills of painting and colour mixing as they paint fairy-tale characters and self-portraits for a jumble sale frieze. Throughout all the activities, children are encouraged to talk about what they see and feel as they communicate their ideas in painting, collage work and role play.

Week 1

Materials around us

Personal, Social and Emotional Development

- During a circle time show children pieces of different materials. Encourage children to describe them and to talk about things and feelings of which they are reminded. (PS2, 6)

- Go on a walk to look for materials in the local environment. Before the walk remind children of routines for safe walking. (PS8, 9, 12)

Communication, Language and Literacy

- Begin to collect words for naming and describing materials. Write the words on pieces of card and place them in boxes covered with the corresponding material. (L8)

- Blindfold children and ask them to take turns to describe a material such as wood, plastic or paper hidden in a feely bag. Encourage them to use as many descriptive words as possible and to guess what their friends are feeling. (L6)

- Give each child a piece of playdough. Encourage them to explore it using only their fingers and to describe what is happening. Scribe their ideas for a playdough poem (see activity opposite). (L7, 11)

Mathematical Development

- Sort objects into hoops, according to the materials from which they are made. Encourage children to name the materials and to count the number of objects in each hoop. (M1, 2, 4)

- Make a rice salad (see activity opposite). (M9)

Knowledge and Understanding of the World

- Look at the materials used in the sorting activity. Discuss what they might be used for. Encourage children to use names such as 'wood' and 'plastic', as well as words for textures and appearance. (K1, 3)

- Look at pictures of homes around the world. Talk about the materials from which they are made. Encourage children to think of reasons why the materials have been used. (K3, 4)

Physical Development

- Enjoy playing with outside toys. Talk about the toys and what they are made of. Ask why they are outside toys. (PD1, 2, 3)

- Set out a circuit of challenges such as throwing a bean bag into a bucket, walking along a wooden bench, rolling across a rubber mat and building a tower with wooden bricks. Again help children to be aware of the materials in the things they use. (PD1, 6)

Creative Development

- Make models with clay. Talk about the way the clay behaves and feels. Leave the models to dry over a week and help children to notice the way the clay changes. (CD1)

- Put out a range of things such as plastic tubs, card boxes, tubes, pipe cleaners, fabrics and straws. Invite children to make props for acting nursery rhymes. (CD4, 5)

- Make a collection of wooden blocks, sponges, plastic cotton reels and other objects suitable for making prints. Enjoy using them with ready-mixed paints on black paper. (CD1)

- Sing 'The wise man built his house upon the rock' from *Okki-tokki-unga Action Songs for Children* chosen by Beatrice Harrop, Linda Friend and David Gadsby (A & C Black). Encourage children to talk about the wise and foolish men and to act out the tale when playing with sand or construction toys. (C4)

Planning for Learning through *What are things made from?*

Practical Pre-School

Activity: Squashy poem

Learning opportunity: Collaborating to make up a poem about playdough.

Early Learning Goal: Creative Development. Children will be able to interact with others, negotiating plans and activities and taking turns in conversation. They will hear and say initial and final sounds in words and short vowels within words.

Resources: For each child a ball of playdough, large sheet of paper, pen.

Organisation: Small group.

Key vocabulary: Playdough, squash, stretch, soft, push, pull, flat, stretch.

What to do:

Give each child a ball of playdough. Ask them to say, in turn, a word to describe how it feels. Write down the words children say. Repeat this for what the playdough looks and smells like. Read back the words to the children starting with the words 'Playdough is ...'. Explain that together you have written a poem. Ask whether they can add any more words to their poem about playdough. Add the new words and read it once more. Finally, let the group enjoy playing with dough.

Repeat the activity with other groups. Write out the poems and make a book of poems about playdough.

Activity: Shape rice salad

Learning opportunity: Collaborating to make a rice salad.

Early Learning Goal: Mathematical Development. Use language such as 'circle' or 'bigger' to describe the shape and size of solids and flat shapes.

Resources: Packet of rice; red and orange peppers; sultanas; red and green seedless grapes; cucumber; apples; pears; clementines; saucepan/microwave bowl; safe knives; chopping boards; set of clean flat and solid shapes; hot plate or microwave; small plastic tubs.

Organisation: Small group.

Key vocabulary: Words for flat and solid shapes, rice, pepper, red, orange.

What to do:

Tell the group that together they are going to make a shape rice salad. Explain that the rice will be cooked, and that when it is cool they will cut the fruits into shapes to put in the rice. Wash hands. Cook the rice according to the instructions on the packet. Involve the group in measuring the water and in counting how many cupfuls of rice are being used. Make sure that children are safe whilst the rice is cooked and that no children touch the rice until it is cool.

Give each child a chopping board and safe knife. Help them to cut the peppers into a variety of shapes. Repeat this with the cucumber, grapes and clementines. As children work, talk to them about shapes. Show them flat and solid shapes such as squares and cubes to compare with the pieces they cut. Finally, help the children to cut the apples and pears into pieces. Roll these pieces in lemon juice to stop them going brown. Together add the chopped pieces to the bowl of cool rice and mix it with a wooden spoon.

Invite children to taste their shape rice salad. Talk about the way the salad was made and the things that the cooking utensils were made from. Divide the remaining rice salad into small plastic tubs for sending home.

Display

Cover a table with sugar paper. Use ribbon or border strip to divide it into six sections labelled 'wood', 'paper', 'card', 'fabric', 'wool' and 'shiny materials'. Over the weeks, invite children to bring from home objects to place on the table in the appropriate section. Where an object is made of more than one material, place it in the section for the material it is mainly made from.

Make a group collage of the prints on black sugar paper. Nearby place the objects used for printing. Encourage children to match the objects to their prints and to notice the difference in the prints made by different materials.

Week 2

Wood

Personal, Social and Emotional Development

- Read *Where's My Teddy?* by Jez Alborough (Walker Books). Talk about why Eddy feels scared in the dark wood. Talk about things that scare children in the group. (PS4, 6)

- Make a collection of objects made from wood. Include both decorative and useful ones such as pencils, wooden spoons, lolly sticks and a recorder. Discuss the way that wood is used to make many things. Talk about the importance of looking after wood. Explain that water will make marks if left on wooden furniture. (PS3, 7)

Communication, Language and Literacy

- Begin a group book box of stories and poems that take place in a wood or forest such as *Where's My Teddy?* by Jez Alborough, 'Little Red Riding Hood' and 'Goldilocks and the Three Bears'. Invite children to add other books to the box and to enjoy sharing them with an adult or other children. (L3)

- As a group use the pictures in *Where's My Teddy?* by Jez Alborough (Walker Books) to retell the story. Make up a new story about Eddy and the Teddy in the woods. Later in the week read the other two stories in the series – *It's the Bear!* and *My Friend Bear*. (L3, 6)

- On a large display board put up a silhouette of a tree with branches. Encourage children to think of words that rhyme with 'wood' and their initial and final sounds. Write the suggested words on paper leaves and display them on the tree. (L11)

Mathematical Development

- Use the counting bricks number rhyme (see activity opposite). (M1, 2, 12)

- Use wooden pencils and cubes to measure lengths and heights. Help children to realise why different pencils may give different answers. (M1, 12)

- Make necklaces and bracelets from colourful wooden beads. Encourage children to make repeating patterns and to count how many beads they have used. (M1, 2, 8)

Knowledge and Understanding of the World

- Use newsprint paper and thick wax crayons to make rubbings of wooden surfaces. Talk about the patterns that are made. Why do different surfaces make different patterns? (K1, 2, 3)

- Enjoy making models with safe off-cuts of wood and lolly sticks. Encourage children to talk about what they will make before they start their models. (K5, 6)

- Look at a wooden xylophone. Help children to realise that the shorter keys make the higher notes. Enjoy tapping pencils or pieces of dowel of varying lengths to hear the sounds they make. Make sure children work safely. Faces should not be near the tapping of wood. (K1, 2, 3)

- Share an apple. Collect and count the pips. Explain that pips are seeds. Plant the pips in a pot of soil. Invite children, each week, to check and water the pips and to notice when leaves appear.

Physical Development

- Show children how to use a wooden bat to hit a small ball upwards ten times. Invite them to try and do the same. (PD6)

- Practise walking along wooden benches. Talk about the need to keep arms outstretched to help children to balance. (PD2)

- Enjoy constructing with wooden bricks. (PD8)

Creative Development

- Enjoy using wooden percussion instruments such as claves, maracas, xylophones and castanets. Invite children to accompany the singing of nursery rhymes and to make up their own tunes and songs. (CD2)

- Make wooden frames for photographs (see activity opposite). (CD3)

● Enjoy painting landscapes on off-cuts of wood. Make sure surfaces are splinter free before painting begins. Encourage children to notice the way paint behaves on wood and the patterns made by the wood grain. (C1)

Activity: Counting bricks number rhyme

Learning opportunity: Enjoying counting with a number rhyme.

Early Learning Goal: Mathematical Development. Children will be able to say and use number names in order in familiar contexts. They will count reliably up to ten everyday objects. They will use language such as 'greater', 'smaller' ... to compare quantities.

Resources: Toy wooden cubes/bricks.

Organisation: Whole group.

Key vocabulary: Wood, block, numbers to ten, shorter, taller.

What to do:

Invite a child to build a tower with five blocks. Explain that the tower will be used in a new rhyme. Recite the rhyme, inserting the name of the child who built the tower. After the final line, as a group, count the blocks.

> (Child's name) has built a tower with blocks of wood,
> We all think that it looks good!
> How many blocks did (child's name) use?
> Let's count and see.

Give another child six blocks to build a tower and repeat the rhyme. On further occasions the first line can be changed to describe the type of tower that is to be made, for example '(child's name) is building a taller/shorter/fatter tower with blocks of wood'.

Activity: Wooden frames

Learning opportunity: Using a camera and making frames with wood.

Early Learning Goal: Creative Development. Children will be able to respond in a variety of ways to what they see.

Resources: Child-friendly camera; lolly sticks cut into 1cm and 2cm pieces; match sticks; felt pens; PVA glue; glue spreaders; thick card; card pieces the same size as the developed photos and some pieces 2cm wider and longer; Blu-tack; double-sided sticky tape.

Organisation: Pairs (to take photos), groups of four children (to make frames).

Key vocabulary: Frame, tree, photo.

What to do:

In the week before 'Wood week' take pairs of children outside to take a photo of a tree or something made from wood. Children might wish to sit on a wooden bench and take a photo of a friend. Explain that next week they will be able to make wooden frames for the photos.

To make the frames use Blu-tack to place a photo-sized piece of card in the centre of a larger piece. Show children how to make small dabs of glue on lolly stick pieces and/or match sticks and press them firmly around the photo-sized card. Explain where the photo will eventually go and that the wooden pieces must not touch the photo-sized card. When completed, remove the photo-sized card and leave the frame to dry over night. Use felt pens to decorate the frame and stick the photo on with double-sided sticky tape. Finally tape loops of ribbon to the backs for hanging the pictures up.

Display

Put up the framed photos on a display board. Invite children to say where they would like their photos to be placed and to make name labels.

Place the pot with apple pips on a table where children can look but not touch. Nearby put out non-fiction books on trees/wood; sealed, transparent pots containing pips from a variety of fruits and a plastic magnifier. Encourage children to notice the difference in the pips and to find pictures of the fruits from which the pips came.

Week 3
Paper and card

Personal, Social and Emotional Development

- During a circle time sort out a bin of clean rubbish into card, paper and other materials. Introduce the idea of recycling. Show children the symbol that shows something has been made from recycled materials. (PS1, 9, 12)

- Invite a member of the local council to come and talk about paper recycling. After the visit, encourage the children to make thank-you cards. (PS1, 2, 3)

Communication, Language and Literacy

- Read *The Jolly Postman or Other People's Letters* by Janet and Allan Ahlberg (Heinemann). Make a group big book of letters to the Jolly Postman (see activity opposite). (L3, 16, 19)

- Set up a role-play post office. Provide a variety of cards, papers and envelopes for children to enjoy 'writing' and posting. (L18, 19)

- Enjoy sharing *Katie Morag Delivers the Mail* by Mairi Hedderwick (Red Fox). (L3)

- Make posters to remind people not to waste paper. (L18, 19)

Mathematical Development

- Use paper and card squares, triangles, rectangles and circles in bright colours to make pictures and patterns. As children make their collages encourage them to talk about the shapes they choose and to notice the differences and similarities. (M9)

- Use old greetings cards and picture postcards for sorting and counting. (M1, 2)

- Play Snap using cards with numbers to ten on them. Help children to recognise the numbers, to count the cards in their piles and to realise why Snap cards need to be made of card and not paper. (M1, 2, 3, 4)

Knowledge and Understanding of the World

- Sort a variety of pieces of card and paper. Help children to consider how they might be used and why. (K1, 3)

- Make a group display of decorations and cards made from paper and/or card used to celebrate festivals by families within the group. Invite carers to come and talk about the celebrations. (K10)

- Use a non-fiction book to show children how paper is made from trees. Help children to understand that trees take time to grow and why it is important not to waste paper. (K4)

Physical Development

- Play the traditional 'flapping fish' game. Cut fish from A4 sized pieces of paper. Use magazines to wave and bang close to the fish to take them for a swim. Once children know how to move their fish, the game can be played as a race to see whose fish arrives first in a hoop. (PD2, 6)

- Set up a slalom circuit with card flags taped onto plastic cones. Give challenges for children to do before you have counted to ten such as dribble a ball, hop, jump or walk balancing a bean bag on the head around the flags. (PD2, 3, 6)

Creative Development

- Make a large patchwork with pieces of scrap paper. Encourage children to bring in scraps from home and to collect as many different pieces as possible. Include pieces from clean paper and card food wrappers as well as papers such as crepe, tissue, sugar and wrapping. (CD1)

- Make masks from paper plates. Provide a range of scrap papers for children to make eyes, ears, hair, beards, hats, and so on. Use the masks for role play. (CD4, 5)

- Paint fairy tale characters who wrote letters delivered by the Jolly Postman. (CD1)

- Provide postcard-sized pieces of card and colourful magazines for making collages (see activity opposite). (CD1)

Activity: Writing to the Jolly Postman

Learning opportunity: Using a pencil. Attempting to write initial and final sounds and simple words.

Early Learning Goal: Communication, Language and Literacy. Children will be able to listen with enjoyment and respond to stories, rhymes and poems. They will attempt writing for various purposes, using features of different forms. They will use a pencil and hold it effectively to form recognisable letters, most of which are correctly formed.

Resources: *The Jolly Postman* or *Other People's Letters* by Janet and Allan Ahlberg (Heinemann); postcards; letter writing paper; envelopes; stamp-sized pieces of paper; pencils; crayons; glue; postbox (made from box painted red).

Organisation: Whole group introduction, small group letter activity.

Key vocabulary: Jolly, postman, stamp, letter, envelope, card.

What to do:

Share *The Jolly Postman* or *Other People's Letters* book. Some groups may wish to read all the letters whilst for others it may be more appropriate to select two or three and read the others on subsequent days. Encourage children to talk about the fairy tale characters that have written the letters and to think about the reasons for writing them. Talk about the Jolly Postman. Does he look jolly? Do children think he likes delivering letters? Does he ever get any? Explain that they have the chance to write to the Jolly Postman.

Divide into small groups. Show children the postcards and letter paper. Help children to write a letter and to read it to the group. When the letters are finished provide envelopes and stamp-sized paper. Finally, post the letters.

The next day, tell children that the postman was so thrilled with the letters that he has sent them a reply. Share a letter from the Jolly Postman that mentions each of the children by name. In the letter say that he enjoyed the letters so much that he has sent them back so that they can be displayed for everyone to read.

Activity: Postcard collages

Learning opportunity: Cutting, tearing and sticking.

Early Learning Goal: Creative Development. Children will explore colour, shape, form and space in two dimensions.

Resources: Postcards showing scenery; old magazines; postcard-sized pieces of stiff card; scissors; pencils; glue.

Organisation: Small group.

Key vocabulary: Tear, stick, cut, words to describe the scenes on the postcards; collage.

What to do:

Show the group the postcards. Encourage them to look closely at the details such as colours, trees, buildings, grass, sea and sky. Then show them the magazines. Ask whether children can find similar colours/details.

Explain that you are going to make a picture using pieces taken from magazines. Ask the children to help you find pieces of blue paper for sky. Demonstrate how to glue pieces cut from the magazines onto the card to make a patchwork sky. Show how pieces can be torn to make clouds, bushes, and so on.

Discuss the kinds of pictures children would like to make. Encourage children to use the magazines to make scenes and to enjoy cutting, tearing and sticking. Remind children that changes can be made simply by gluing new pieces of paper on top.

Display

Cover a display board with sky coloured paper. Display the letters to the Jolly Postman. Place some in envelopes at child height for them to take out, 'read' and replace. Stick others slightly curving from the board for a three-dimensional effect. Put up the painted, fairy tale characters around the board. Place the Jolly Postman books and the postbox on a nearby table. Provide more paper and envelopes for children to enjoy writing and posting letters.

Week 4

Fabric and wool

Personal, Social and Emotional Development

- During a circle time talk about the importance of looking after clothes. Encourage children to think about the need to hang up coats. Demonstrate how to fold clothes. (PS9)

- Provide a range of clothes for children to enjoy folding and for dressing up. (PS10)

- Make 'I can …' concertina books for dressing and looking after clothes (see activity opposite). (PS10)

Communication, Language and Literacy

- Read *The Queen's Knickers* by Nicholas Allan (Red Fox). Talk about the kinds of knickers worn by the queen. Which ones did children like best? (L3)

- Look at feely books made for young children, for example *Spot's Touch and Feel Book* by Eric Hill (Penguin) and *Usborne Touchy Feely Diggers* by Fiona Watt (Usborne). Make a group feely book. Encourage children to make a feely picture using pieces of fabric and to 'write'/think of a sentence. (L16, 17)

- Enjoy reciting 'Baa baa black sheep'. As a group think of different materials to replace the word 'wool' and new answers, for example:

  Baa baa black sheep,

  Have you any wood?

  Yes sir, yes sir,

  It's really good! (L3)

Mathematical Development

- Use lengths of wool to measure and compare the heights of a range of objects/shapes. (M9, 12)

- Make a collection of pieces of patterned fabric. Use the fabrics for counting activities and shape recognition, for example which pieces have two colours? Which piece has more than seven spots? Point to the squares. (M1, 2)

- Show children a tartan kilt. Use rectangles and squares of sticky paper to make new tartans. (M8)

Knowledge and Understanding of the World

- Design new knickers for the queen (see activity opposite). (K6)

- Use magnifiers to observe and compare fabrics. (K1, 3)

- Make flags by stapling fabric to 30cm pieces of wood. Place the flags in draughty areas where children can safely watch the flags blowing. Do different fabrics move in different ways? Which fabrics make the best flags? Why? (K1, 2, 4)

Physical Development

- Use fabric bands in a variety of colours for children to wear whilst enjoying taking part in simple races. (PD1, 2, 3)

- Use bean bags and hoops to practise throwing, catching and aiming at targets. (PD6)

Creative Development

- Provide large pieces of fabric in a range of

colours for children to use for role play. Encourage them to use the fabrics in different ways, for costumes, scenery (sea, mountain, grass and so on) and props. (CD4, 5))

● Enjoy weaving with thin strips of fabric or thick wool. (CD1)

Activity: Making 'I can' books

Learning opportunity: Making books to record children's success in dressing/undressing.

Early Learning Goal: Personal, Social and Emotional Development. Children will dress and undress independently.

Resources: Concertina books with eight sections and 'I can' written at the top of each page (one for each child); pencils; crayons; selection of children's clothes

Organisation: Whole group.

Key vocabulary: Dress, undress, fasten, fold, right side out, names of articles of clothing.

What to do:

Show children the pile of clothes. Ask whether anyone knows how to fasten buttons. Invite a child to demonstrate how to put on a cardigan and fasten a button. Invite other children to choose different items of clothes to put on.

Show children the 'I can' books. Explain that there is a book for each child and that they will draw pictures of all the clothes that they can put on alone. Encourage children to talk about getting dressed in the morning. Do they put on their own socks? Who knows how to fasten their shoes? Give out the books. Ask children to draw and colour pictures of clothes they are able to put on without help. Some children may also wish to write words or initial sounds to complete the sentence 'I can …'.

Activity: Designing knickers for the queen

Learning opportunity: Designing and making.

Early Learning Goal: Knowledge and Understanding of the World. Children will be able to select tools and techniques they need to shape, assemble and join the materials they are using.

Resources: Range of papers and fabrics; PVA glue; spreaders; A4 paper; pencils; *The Queen's Knickers* by Nicholas Allan (Red Fox).

Organisation: Whole group introduction, small group for the activity.

Key vocabulary: Queen, knickers.

What to do:

Read *The Queen's Knickers* by Nicholas Allan. As a group, look at the pictures. Which knickers do the children like best? Why? Which ones would the queen find most useful?

Provide paper, pencils and scraps of paper and fabrics for small groups to make new knickers for the queen. Encourage children to draw a shape for the knickers and to stick scraps on. When finished, ask children to think of an occasion/time when the queen might use the knickers.

Display

Display the new tartan designs on a board alongside a table of sample tartan fabrics - a travel rug, a kilt, a scarf. Collect and display some samples of wool in different forms - raw sheep's wool (washed), a ball of knitting wool, a woolly jumper, woollen fabric - for children to touch and feel.

Week 5
Shiny materials

Personal, Social and Emotional Development

- Use *The Rainbow Fish* by Marcus Pfister (North South Books) for discussion about the importance of sharing. Cut scales from holographic paper to share with children for making rainbow fish. (PS8)

- Prepare a basket of shiny objects such as a key, a plastic mirror and a necklace. Invite children to select a shiny object and to say why they chose it. Encourage children to describe special times when the object might be important. (PS2,4)

Communication, Language and Literacy

- Tell children the story of 'Snow White'. Provide large plastic mirrors for children to join in with the parts where the wicked queen talks to the mirror. As a group, write new responses to answer 'Mirror, mirror on the wall, Who is the fairest one of all?' (L3)

- Enjoy sharing other stories about the rainbow fish. Begin a collection of words that have 'sh' in them. (L2)

- Encourage children to use crayons in metallic colours for writing activities. (L18, 19)

Mathematical Development

- Make stars with wooden lolly sticks. Decorate them with glitter, sequins and shiny scraps. Hang them in a draughty area. (M1, 9)

- Prepare circles of stiff card, each with a number on from one to six. Ask children to stick on shiny stars or sequins for the corresponding number. (M2, 3)

- Use a fish and shiny scales cut from card to practise adding and subtracting (see activity opposite). (M2, 6)

Knowledge and Understanding of the World

- Provide concave, convex and flat plastic mirrors for children to observe and describe their reflections. (K1)

- Investigate the sounds that can be made by tapping shiny spoons in a variety of shapes and sizes. Which spoons make the loudest/highest sounds? (K1, 3)

- Investigate the best way to polish two pence coins, for example dry duster, wet cloth, vinegar, cotton wool. Who can make the shiniest coin? (K1, 3)

Physical Development

- Encourage children to move with control as they pretend to be mirrors and copy movements of adults and friends. (PD2)

- Make a magnetic fishing game with shiny fish. (PD6)

Creative Development

- Make shiny jewellery (see activity opposite). (CD1)

- Enjoy using shiny percussion instruments such as triangles, tambourines, bells and glockenspiels. (CD2)

- Use shiny materials and cardboard tubes to make models of candles. Add glitter for an extra shiny effect. (CD1)

Activity: Counting with the rainbow fish

Learning opportunity: Using numbers to ten and finding one more/less.

Early Learning Goal: Mathematical Development. Children will be able to count reliably up to ten everyday objects. They will find one more or one less than a number from one to ten.

Resources: A large fish cut from blue card; shell or stone shape cut from card, large enough to cover the fish; ten shiny card scales; *The Rainbow Fish* by Marcus Pfister (North South Books).

Organisation: Small group.

Key vocabulary: Rainbow, fish, scales, less, more, numbers to ten, How many?

What to do:

Show children the pictures in *The Rainbow Fish*. Encourage children to look closely, to count fish and scales and to compare the numbers of shiny scales on the rainbow fish as it swims through the book.

Show the group the card fish and the scales. Ask a child to place two scales on the fish. Cover the fish with the shell. Ask 'How many scales has the fish got?' Remove one scale. Ask 'How many scales are on the fish now?' Remove the shell and show the one scale. Repeat this with other numbers of scales. Encourage children to shut their eyes and to picture the fish and the scales.

Activity: Shiny jewellery

Learning opportunity: Cutting and sticking.

Early Learning Goal: Creative Development. Children will be able to explore shape, form and space in two or three dimensions.

Resources: Foil; shapes cut from thick pieces of card; glue; sequins; card circles (the insides of coffee jar lids are ideal); collection of cheap, shiny jewellery (check for sharp edges).

Organisation: Small group.

Key vocabulary: Shiny, jewellery, brooch, necklace.

What to do:

Show children the shiny jewellery. Ask them who might wear the jewellery and why. Do the children like wearing jewellery? Explain that they are going to make jewellery out of foil and card.

Show the group the pieces of card, foil and sequins. Demonstrate how to stick small pieces of card onto a card circle. When the glue is dry press a piece of foil tightly over the jewellery. Make sure that it is smooth and tight so that the outlines of the shapes under the foil can be seen. Fasten the foil with tape on the back. Sequins can be added for an extra shiny effect.

Display

Hang the shiny number circles and rainbow fish in a draughty area . Cover a table with blue or silver shiny paper and set out the Rainbow Fish books. Invite children to bring safe shiny objects from home to go on the table. Remember to check with parents and carers that they are happy for the objects to be displayed.

Week 6

The jumble sale

Personal, Social and Emotional Development

- Introduce the idea of the jumble sale. As a group, decide what the money raised will be for. Discuss the types of job that will need to be done to prepare for the jumble sale. (PS8)

- During a circle time discuss the importance of saying please and thank you. (PS4, 9)

Communication, Language and Literacy

- Explain that each stall will be for a type of material such as fabric, wool, shiny materials, card and paper, glass and china, plastic, and so on. Ask children for ideas for the stalls, encouraging them to think about the types of things they might collect to sell. Make signs for the stalls. (L5, 17)

- Make posters to advertise the jumble sale (see activity opposite). (L18, 19)

- Make a big book about preparations for the sale. (L16, 17, 18)

Mathematical Development

- Involve children in making biscuits, buns and chocolate crispy cakes to sell at the sale. Help them to measure out the ingredients and to count out sweets for decorating the cooked buns and biscuits. (M1, 2, 12)

- Explain that everything at the jumble sale will cost 10 or 20 pence. Introduce children to the coins. Talk about their shapes. Count the number of sides on a 20 pence coin. Set up a role-play shop and provide 10 and 20 pence coins for children to use. (M1, 9)

- Write on pieces of card the names of people who will be invited to the sale. As a group, sort the people and count how many are in each group. Categories might include mummies, daddies and childminders; or people whose names begin with particular letters. (M1, 2, 4)

Knowledge and Understanding of the World

- Make a collection of carrier bags. Help children to notice the differences and similarities in the bags. Which would be best for carrying heavy items? Which would be good to use in wet weather? (K3)

- Investigate what is best to use for waterproof poster writing. Compare pencils, wax and pencil crayons, chalk and paint. (K3)

- Invite a shopkeeper or someone who sells at car boot sales to talk to the group about buying and selling. Afterwards, encourage children to make thank-you cards. (K2)

- Involve children in using a digital camera to take photos for the group's big book about the sale. (K7)

Physical Development

- Tell a story for children to mime going to a jumble sale (see activity opposite). (PD1, 2)

- Enjoy dressing-up races. After the races, help children to notice the changes in their bodies such as red faces and faster breathing. (PD2, 3, 5)

Creative Development

- Provide the range of materials used over previous weeks for children to enjoy making models of their own choosing. (CD1)

- After the jumble sale, encourage children to paint pictures of their favourite part. (CD1)

- Make a group frieze of the jumble sale. Ask children to paint self-portraits. Display the portraits as children buying or selling. Staple real clothes on to a stall for the portraits to sell. (CD1)

Activity: Jumble sale posters

Learning opportunity: Making posters.

Early Learning Goal: Communication, Language and Literacy. Children will be able to use their phonic knowledge to write simple regular words and make phonetically plausible attempts at more complex words. They will use a pencil and hold it effectively to form recognisable letters, most of which are formed correctly.

Resources: A3 sheets of white paper; crayons; pencils; a poster for a children's event.

Organisation: Whole group but with individual help for the writing.

Key vocabulary: Jumble sale, poster, come.

What to do:

Show children a poster for a children's event. Explain that posters advertise things. Ask what the poster is advertising. Can children find any words/letters on the poster? Talk about the need for posters to be clear, easy to see/read and use colours that encourage people to read them.

Explain that posters will be needed to advertise the group's jumble sale. Talk about the kinds of things that would need to go on the posters. What might children draw? Hand out the paper and ask children to draw pictures on their posters.

Once pictures have been drawn and coloured work with individuals for the writing part. Check children's pencil grips. Encourage them to write letters/words and check the letter formation. Use talk and demonstration to help children to form letters correctly.

Activity: Going to the jumble sale

Learning opportunity: Moving with control and imagination.

Early Learning Goal: Physical Development. Children will be able to move with confidence, imagination and in safety. They will move with control and co-ordination.

Resources: Large space; benches.

Organisation: Whole group.

Key vocabulary: Jumble sale, stall, pay, buy, sell, change.

What to do:

Tell the children they are going to go to a jumble sale. Encourage them to move and mime as you describe the journey to get to the sale. Go over bridges (benches), through a tunnel, on a bus and walk in the rain through the puddles. At the sale encourage children to buy clothes and toys and eat refreshments before returning home carrying heavy bags. Finally, talk to children about the stalls at which they bought things.

Display

Put up the posters where they can be easily seen. Encourage visitors to read the posters so that children see them being used.

After the jumble sale has taken place, make a group frieze of children selling and buying. Place the paintings of children's favourite jumble sale parts in clear plastic wallets to make a big book. Place this on a nearby table along with the one about the sale preparations.

Bringing it all together

The jumble sale

A jumble sale is a practical opportunity for children to sort items according to the materials from which they are made. Children will enjoy helping to get ready for the sale and buying and selling items.

Preparation

At the start of the topic, tell carers about the forthcoming jumble sale. Explain that the stalls will be sorted according to what materials the items for sale are made from and that they will cost either 10 or 20 pence. Ask carers who come to the sale to bring only 10 pence or 20 pence coins so that children can easily help with the selling and counting of money at the end. Invite them to donate items to sell that children would like to buy.

With children sort the items collected into stalls such as fabric, wool, shiny materials, card and paper, glass and china and plastic. Then sort the items into things that cost 10 pence and things that will be sold for 20 pence. Encourage children to say why they have chosen a particular price. Discuss how the money raised might be used.

Food

Involve children in preparing refreshments for the jumble sale. Buns, biscuits and chocolate crispy cakes are always popular and provide valuable opportunities for children to count, estimate and measure. Help children to wash and count grapes and cherry tomatoes into small plastic beakers.

The jumble sale

Organise children into small groups, each with an adult helper. As a group, set out a stall. Make sure children know how much the items cost and what the items for sale are made from. Remind children how to greet a customer and to say please and thank you. Act out being a stall holder and a customer.

Hold the jumble sale for the final hour of a normal group session. Arrange times for children to serve on their stall and times for them to be customers with their carers.

Resources

Resources to collect

- Ingredients for making a rice salad (rice, red and orange peppers, cucumber, apples, grapes, clementines, pears, grapes, lemon juice).

- Safe knives and chopping boards.

- Objects made from wood.

- Wooden percussion instruments.

- Items for a role-play post office, for example post box, cash register, envelopes, stamps.

Everyday resources

- Large and small boxes for modelling.

- Papers and cards of different weights, colours and textures, such as sugar paper, corrugated card, silver and shiny papers.

- Dry powder paints for mixing and mixed paints.

- Different sized paint brushes from household brushes to thin brushes for delicate work and a variety of paint mixing containers.

- A variety of drawing and colouring pencils, crayons, pastels, and so on.

- Additional decorative and finishing materials such as sequins, foils, glitter, tinsel, shiny wool and threads, beads, pieces of textiles, and parcel ribbon.

- Table covers.

- Lolly sticks, match sticks and off-cuts of wood.

- Clay.

Stories

The Queen's Knickers by Nicholas Allan (Red Fox).

The Jolly Postman or *Other People's Letters* by Janet and Allan Ahlberg (Heinemann).

The Jolly Christmas Postman by Janet and Allan Ahlberg (Heinemann).

The Jolly Pocket Postman by Janet and Allan Ahlberg (Heinemann).

Where's My Teddy? by Jez Alborough (Walker Books).

It's the Bear! by Jez Alborough (Walker Books).

My Friend Bear by Jez Alborough (Walker Books).

Katie Morag Delivers the Mail by Mairi Hedderwick (Red Fox).

Spot's Touch and Feel Book by Eric Hill (Penguin).

Fairy tales from the *Ladybird Favourite Tales* collection: *Goldilocks and the Three Bears; Little Red Riding Hood*.

The Rainbow Fish by Marcus Pfister (North South Books).

Rainbow Fish and the Big Blue Whale by Marcus Pfister (North South Books).

Rainbow Fish to the Rescue by Marcus Pfister (North South Books).

Usborne Touchy Feely Diggers by Fiona Watt (Usborne).

Songs

Okki-tokki-unga Action Songs for Children chosen by Beatrice Harrop, Linda Friend and David Gadsby (A and C Black).

Collecting evidence of children's learning

Monitoring children's development is an important task. Keeping a record of children's achievements will help you to see progress and will draw attention to those who are having difficulties for some reason. If a child needs additional professional help, such as speech therapy, your records will provide valuable evidence.

Records should be the result of collaboration between group leaders, parents and carers. Parents should be made aware of your record keeping policies when their child joins your group. Show them the type of records you are keeping and make sure they understand that they have an opportunity to contribute. As a general rule, your records should form an open document. Any parent should have access to records relating to his or her child. Take regular opportunities to talk to parents about children's progress. If you have formal discussions regarding children about whom you have particular concerns, a dated record of the main points should be kept.

Keeping it manageable

Records should be helpful in informing group leaders, adult helpers and parents and always be for the benefit of the child. However, keeping records of every aspect of each child's development can become a difficult task. The sample shown will help to keep records manageable and useful. The golden rule is to keep them simple.

Observations will basically fall into three categories:

● **Spontaneous records:** Sometimes you will want to make a note of observations as they happen, for example a child is heard counting cars accurately during a play activity, or is seen to play collaboratively for the first time.

● **Planned observations:** Sometimes you will plan to make observations of children's developing skills in their everyday activities. Using the learning opportunity identified for an activity will help you to make appropriate judgments about children's capabilities and to record them systematically.

To collect information:

● talk to children about their activities and listen to their responses;

● listen to children talking to each other;

● observe children's work such as early writing, drawings, paintings and 3-d models. (Keeping photocopies or photographs is sometimes useful.)

Sometimes you may wish to set up one-off activities for the purposes of monitoring development. Some groups, for example, ask children to make a drawing of themselves at the beginning of each term to record their progressing skills in both coordination and observation. Do not attempt to make records following every activity!

● **Reflective observations:** It is useful to spend regular time reflecting on the progress of a few children (about four children each week). Aim to make some brief comments about each child every half term.

Informing your planning

Collecting evidence about children's progress is time-consuming but essential. When you are planning, use the information you have collected to help you to decide what learning opportunities you need to provide next for children. For example, a child who has poor pencil or brush control will benefit from more play with dough or construction toys to build the strength of hand muscles.

Example of recording chart

Name: Rosie Conmay		D.O.B. 1.2.98			Date of entry: 13.9.02	
Term	Personal, Social and Emotional Development	Communication, Language and Literacy	Mathematical Development	Knowledge and Understanding of the World	Physical Development	Creative Development
ONE	Happy to say good-bye to mother. Enjoys collaborative play. 20.9.01 EMH	Enjoys listening to stories. Particularly enjoys rhymes. Can write first name. Good pencil grip. 20.10.01 EMH	Is able to say numbers to ten and count accurately five objects. Recognises and names squares and circles. 5.11.01EH	Very eager to ask questions. Loves to carry out experiments. Able to distinguish and name materials. 16.10.01 AC	Can balance on one leg. Loved miming going to jumble sale. Does not like feel of playdough. 16.10.01 AC	Loves glitter and glue! Enjoys painting, mixing own colours. 16.10.01 LSS
TWO						
THREE						

Planning for Learning through What are things made from?

Practical Pre-School

Skills overview of six-week plan

	Topic focus	Personal, Social and Emotional Development	Communication, Language and Literacy	Mathematical Development	Knowledge and Understanding of the World	Physical Development	Creative Development
1	Materials around us	Listening Expressing emotions Understanding what is right and wrong	Listening; Writing Recognising initial and final sounds; Extending vocabulary	Counting; Sorting Comparing; Recognition of shapes	Making observations Comparing; Talking; Naming materials	Moving with control; Using outside toys; Aiming and throwing; Balancing	Using clay; Constructing Printing; Singing
2	Wood	Listening Understanding what is right and wrong Talking about feelings	Listening; Responding to stories; Recognising initial and final sounds	Counting; Measuring lengths; Making patterns	Comparing; Describing Investigating; Sticking	Moving with control and in safety; Balancing Construction; Using small equipment	Painting; Sticking; Singing Playing percussion instruments
3	Paper and card	Showing interest Maintaining attention Speaking Understanding what is right and wrong Considering consequences	Writing; Role play Listening and responding to stories	Sorting; Counting Recognising numbers Using shapes	Comparing; Investigating Asking questions; Talking about celebrations	Moving with control and co-ordination; Showing awareness of space, themselves and others Using small equipment	Making masks; Role play Collage
4	Fabric and wool	Understand what is right and wrong and why Dressing and undressing independently Taking care of clothes	Responding to a story and a rhyme; Making feely books; Speaking	Counting; Measuring heights; Making patterns; Recognising shapes; Comparing	Designing; Observing Comparing; Asking questions Selecting tools and techniques	Moving with control, co-ordination and in safety Throwing, catching and aiming	Role play; Making costumes and props Weaving; Collage
5	Shiny materials	Listening; Speaking Being aware of others' feelings	Responding to a story Writing; Collecting words with 'sh'	Counting; Recognising numbers; Using shapes	Investigating; Observing Describing; Talking	Moving with control; Using small and large equipment	Cutting and sticking Playing percussion instruments
6	The jumble sale	Awareness of others Saying please and thank you; Collaborative planning	Making a big book, posters and signs; Speaking	Baking; Counting Recognising coins; Role play, shopping and selling	Observing; Comparing; Using a camera; Asking questions Talking	Moving with imagination, coordination and in safety Recognising changes in bodies after activity	Painting; Making models

Home links

The theme of 'What are things made from?' lends itself to useful links with children's homes and families. Through working together children and adults gain respect for each other and build comfortable and confident relationships.

Establishing partnerships

- Keep parents informed about the topic of 'What are things made from?' and the themes for each week. By understanding the work of the group, parents will enjoy the involvement of contributing ideas, time and resources.

- Photocopy the parent's page for each child to take home.

- Invite friends, childminders and families to the jumble sale.

Visiting enthusiasts

- Invite adults to come to the group to talk about buying and selling at car boot sales and jumble sales. What types of things have they bought/sold? What were they made from?

Resource requests

- Ask parents to contribute left-over wallpaper, remnants of fabric, wool or shiny materials that could be used for collages, model making and sorting activities.

- Catalogues, greetings cards and colour supplement magazines are invaluable for collage work and a wide range of interesting activities.

The jumble sale

- It is always useful to have extra adults at times such as the jumble sale.

- Ask parents to contribute items to sell and refreshments, for example fruit, biscuits and popcorn.

- Invite a parent with a video camera to make a record of the jumble sale to share with children.